This book is dedicated to my older sister, Karen Charnigo, who biked and rode the train with me in Cuyahoga Valley National Park. She is so fortunate to live only a few miles away from the park.

The train is coming
for you and for me.

You can ride it for miles
and bring your bike too.
A trip through the valley -
so much fun for you.

Come visit the park
and ride the train there.
On the bridge to Beaver
Marsh, at the wetlands you'll
stare.

Or hop on a bike

And ride on the trail.

You're sure to see nature

without any fail.

Take a close look.
What do you see?

It's the train depot.
Will you wait with me?

Take a close look.
What do you see?

It's a pump to
get water.
Are you
thirsty?

Look for other National Park books by Dr. Josie Zayac

- A Close Up Look at Bryce Canyon National Park
- A Close Up Look at Crater Lake National Park
- A Close Up Look at Cuyahoga Valley National Park
- A Close Up Look at Joshua Tree National Park
- A Close Up Look at Redwood National and State Parks
- A Close Up Look at Rocky Mountain National Park
- A Close Up Look at Sequoia National Park
- A Close Up Look at Theodore Roosevelt National Park
- A Close Up Look at Zion National Park

Facts about Cuyahoga Valley National Park, Ohio

- Established as a recreational area in 1974
- Became a National Park in 2000
- Includes 33,000 acres of land along 22 miles of river
- Beaver Marsh, a former junk yard, was cleaned up by the community
- Beavers had been gone for over 100 years and returned once the area was cleaned up

Take a close look.
What do you see?

Some swallowtail butterflies, so pretty to me.

Take a close look.
What do you see?

On top of the thistle,
I see a bee.

Take a close look.
What do you see?

I see some fungus,
growing on a tree.

Take a close look.
What do you see?

It's a few buckeyes, From Ohio's state tree.

The buckeye tree has been the state tree since 1953.

Take a close look.
What's to be seen?

A beautiful heron.
This one is green.

It's a great blue heron
Getting ready to flee.

This majestic bird's wings
are seven feet wide.
It's the largest heron.
Good thing it's outside!

Take a close look.

What do you see?

Take a close look.
What do you see?

I see a turtle sunning
on a fallen tree.

Take a close look.
What do you see?

I see a bullfrog
here on a lily.

Locks were used in days gone by. They moved a boat from low to high.

Take a close look.
What do you see?

I see a piece of machinery.

Cuyahoga Valley National Park
is a great place to play.
Cuyahoga means "crooked";
the river flows that way!

A Close Up Look at

Cuyahoga Valley National Park

By Josie Zayac